soft sift

MARK FORD

soft sift

HARCOURT, INC.

Orlando ★ Austin ★ New York ★ San Diego ★ Toronto ★ London

www.HarcourtBooks.com

Library of Congress Cataloging-in-Publication Data

Ford, Mark, 1962–

Soft Sift / Mark Ford.—1st U.S. ed.

p. cm.

ISBN: 0-15-100949-X

I. Title.

PR6106.O74 S6 2003

821'.92—dc21

2002038705

First published in the United Kingdom
by Faber and Faber Limited

Text set in Dante
Designed by Scott Piehl

Printed in the United States of America

First U.S. edition

A C E G I H F D B

For Kate

FOREWORD

Ever since I first happened on Mark Ford's poetry, some fifteen years ago, it has struck me that it is a kind of poetry unlike any other being written in English. This may be in part because of his having been brought up in various parts of the world. Born in Nairobi in 1962, Ford also spent time in Nigeria, Sri Lanka, Hong Kong, Bahrain, and the United States, where his father was posted for ten years. He spent two years in Japan as a visiting professor at the University of Kyoto. One might have expected to see repercussions of this stay in his poetry, but he has said that during that time he produced only ten lines—the beginning of "Looping the Loop," the first poem in *Soft Sift*, though he feels that "my experiences of Japanese landscapes and cities, culture and poetry, sift softly through the entire collection." By way of explanation he cites a famous haiku of Buson: "A tethered horse/ snow/ in both stirrups." Such are the devious ways of influence, and it would be wrong to measure Japan's importance in his work by the quantity of lines produced there.

Not that it sounds particularly Japanese. But then, how *does* it sound? To the English I imagine it sounds American, perhaps because of the occasional dash of U.S. local color (mentions of the Pulaski skyway and Grandma sitting on the front porch with her hound dog, though she appears in the lines written in Japan!), or an occasional New York School riff ("A Swimming-Pool Full of Peanuts" is the title of the longest poem in his first book, *Landlocked*.) Maybe it's the continual determination to experiment with words, which is certainly not a trait of most contemporary British poetry. But Ford's tense, deliberate experimentation isn't American either: its seriousness, though little else about it, connects it to Larkin and his disciples, rather than to the anxious glitter of early Auden and prewar British poetry, when camp and politics co-existed somewhat uneasily. Neither element, as far as I can tell, plays much of a role in Ford's work.

One important influence is certainly that of the French novelist and poet Raymond Roussel (1877–1933), on whom Ford has written the definitive study in English (*Raymond Roussel and the Republic of Dreams*), and whose works are the product of experiments of an almost forbidding intensity. (Roussel was a wealthy recluse whose means allowed him to devote almost his entire life to his writing. Though he attracted the attention of the Dadaists and the Surrealists, the attraction wasn't mutual, and their nihilistic playfulness has no parallel in his work). Ford has written: "I think of the extreme formal rigor—or rather, varieties of rigor—of the poems in *Soft Sift* as analogous to Roussel's compositional methods. It came to seem to me as if words, experiences, could only ever hope to enter the looking glass realm of art by first passing through some narrow, predetermined aperture like that of Roussel's *procédé* [a stratagem, too complicated to summarize here, that Roussel devised by replacing words with their homophones]—or that of the rondeau, the haiku, the sonnet, the couplet, the eight line stanza, or whatever. Emily Dickinson makes a related point in the lines used as an epigraph to Part II of this book: 'And through a Riddle, at the last—/Sagacity, must go—'"

Thus the path to the "looking glass realm of art"—and how courageously right he is to locate the realm of art there, despite those who would insist that bloody chunks of reality should be transferred directly to the page, like meat to the butcher's waxed paper—is a *porte étroite*, a narrow way through which life is transformed into poetry by a process something like dying.

Alice's looking glass is reached via Emily's riddle. And only then can we take the measure of life, after it has been transformed into its opposite, its reflection—more real, it turns out, than the expectant viewer posted in front of the mirror. The riddle is not a game, but a dead-serious operation which is sagacity's only chance of being reborn—as enlightenment—in the poem. The paths to this outcome can seem as devious, or irrelevant, as a translation of a fragment of the remote Apuleius or the delicate Charles d'Orléans. It takes a poet to uncover these unlikely trails, and we recognize him by the results of his search, the "beast in view." Ford's poetry is the real right thing; it matters little how it came to be that.

When I said that Roussel's writing is devoid of playfulness, I didn't mean that it lacks humor. Humor is a central element in his work and also in Ford's, but it is of a peculiar kind, the by-product of an extreme seriousness that's not without overtones of lugubriousness. Roussel wrote that he sometimes spent an entire day trying to compose a single sentence. In practice this could mean trying to get rid of a single superfluous word: succinctness was perhaps his chief esthetic concern, but it was a highly verbose concentrate that resulted, leaving one to guess at all that had been left out so as to arrive at writing that has an incredible specific gravity. The monumentality of what has been left out is the key to the humor. In his novel *Impressions d'Afrique*, Roussel describes a prisoner whose punishment is to weave mosquito-traps with his foot out of gossamer-fine filaments of fruit while reciting an enormously long mantra, which is not unlike the tasks Roussel imposed on himself: ridiculously complicated but often culminating in a thing of bizarre beauty, and, in this case, usefulness, that couldn't have been achieved by simpler means. And of course there is something funny about such a contraption. Ford's methods are simpler but no less awe-inspiring, and they somehow leave one feeling good, which is after all what poetry should do. His grotesque self-portrait as a "green amphibian" slithering along the floor of a department store and out the door (in *Landlocked*'s "Outing") has morphed into darker and more realist grotesques in *Soft Sift*, like "the errant protagonist" in "Brinkmanship." But diagnosing and describing a hitherto unknown form of pain can produce invigorating aftershocks. He is locating and enlarging on new kinds of living that we recognize, in the looking glass world, as what we have been doing all along without realizing it. And he does so with superb grace, generosity and wit.

—John Ashbery

CONTENTS

Foreword   vii

PART I

Chaque puzzle de Winckler était pour Bartlebooth une aventure nouvelle, unique, irremplaçable. Chaque fois, il avait l'impression, après avoir brisé les sceaux qui fermaient la boîte noire de Madame Hourcade et étalé sur le drap de sa table, sous la lumière sans ombre du scialytique, les sept cent cinquante petits morceaux de bois qu'étaient devenue son aquarelle, que toute l'expérience qu'il accumulait depuis cinq, dix, ou quinze ans ne lui servirait à rien, qu'il aurait, comme chaque fois, affaire à des difficultés qu'il ne pouvait même pas soupçonner.

Georges Perec, *La Vie mode d'emploi*

LOOPING THE LOOP

Anything can be forgotten, become regular
As newspapers hurled in a spinning arc to land
With a thump on the porch where Grandma sits
And knits, her hound dog yawning at her feet.

And other strangled details will emerge and prove
Suddenly potent to confound the wary-footed, and even
The assembled members of the panel; in turn
Each pundit speaks, yanks from the hat an angry rabbit who
    flops

In spurts around the circular paths of crazy paving.
No pressing need to watch them but you do.

    *

Dirty fingernails in August, and just
The amount of lightning threatened; superb
Courtiers sweep through the various precincts
Fingering each other's beads in the jagged dusk.

I myself went and left like a moron, but heard
The rumours nevertheless — meanwhile the wind
Pounds this shack with wilful abandon, then inquires,
As it eases, just exactly how many spliffs there were

Stashed that night in the cicada-coloured
Pencil case tucked in the side pocket of her satchel.

    *

Harsh truths indeed! I act the part of my own
Nemesis, polite, dazed, addicted to adversity,
Frequently drunk. Overhead the wires hum
Obscure ultimatums, mutterings that threaten

To aggravate forever these ordinary feelings, and inflict
Upon the world quantities of crazily-worded postcards
Sent off on impulse from decaying seaside towns. For I still
Love the tang of brine, the old women hurtling on
    motorbikes

Through swirling banks of fog, any who loiter
Resentfully about the war memorial on summer afternoons.

   ★

Eventually one hears the cuckoo's call, while friends
Recline in armchairs. Let's off then, backwards through
The fish-eye lens, bone by bone, clean shirts
Soon streaked and torn. Some fought like lovers

Under the bluish lights that swayed so weirdly
On their stanchions of pale, unpainted metal; how
Suddenly the team began to perform as if a stranger
Watched and cared, blindly probing through the endless rain

For openings, reeling back aghast, bitterly dispersed
One dank October, the sediment settling as best it might.

   ★

Afloat on the flood, indifferent to the cries
And the silence, I imprison your wandering hand:
In it lurk anecdote and polemic entwined, scars
Faint as a plate's, the luck of the stars ...

Yet the affect hardly emerges, peers forth
Like a strayed mole through a cliff-crevice
On the unfamiliar scene; though I have leapt and held
And carried, grimaced sourly at the brimming heavens,

A few feints and the incident spirals
Beyond reach, turns turtle in dreams displaced before
     morning.

PLAN NINE

The dreadful telephone again: gentle as a kitchen
He'd walk through snow to lay his wreath or convey
Misgivings. The signal fades, freeing me to crawl
Through cold Friday, to forage amid the shadows cast
By a reckless crowd of brittle soap-opera characters.
Our bodies drag, halt mesmerized, lurch forward
With a yelp. 'What's the story, morning glory?'
Inquires the super, whose reign of terror
And mind like glue leave less than ever
To be desired. I drink my Rhenish, though it tastes
Of poison, and attack with everything
Until at last the bugle sounds. Briskly, beyond
These streaming drapes, a caustic voice unfolds the case
To a clutch of bright-eyed interns: no mohair, no alcohol,
Lots of plain yogurt certainly, no foreign languages, no
    tête-à-têtes.

THE GREAT DIVIDE

The teapot slips from the hand. Some
Muscular ache lies patterned on the floor in irregular
Fragments of china; beyond, through the narrow meshes
Of twilight, children's shriekings filter and drain.

Raw fingers' ends search the delicate scalp.
Can these be stray traces of argument
Lost forever to posterity, while delays
And distractions alternate like chequered shade?

In an ill-fitting suit, heart pounding, one
Frowns at the herald's summons. Nothing moves,
Though a fleck still troubles the eye that absorbs
The scene, the shards, the gaudy colours of formica.

CONTINGENCY PLANS

On balance it wasn't so much the cash
I was owed, as the attacks on my character; I
Prayed for deliverance and revenge. November
Lingered on gloomily: colds and fevers swept
The population, reduced swathes to troubled brooding
And red, streaming eyes; in a quandary I seized
My innate Englishness, and practised
Wrapping it around me like an old army coat.

Two strikes, it was decreed, and you were out: appeals
For clemency were received with merry scorn.
As the gridlock eased I changed the subject,
Knowing my father, knowing the trees and the turnings and
        the signs
Along the route, and remembering his aversion to all
Blockages; I felt the engine growl, then
Shudder and forget itself. 'I'm a Rhinestone
Cowboy' rode bucking and spangled across the airwaves
That spread like contours above the country's bumps
And hollows. A buzzing, roving helicopter eyed
The progress of our orderly parade: it would swoop
When necessary, a featherless scavenger lured by carrion.

BEYOND THE BOULEVARD

He merely flapped when we steamed by, then settled
To his accounts; we were all dressed in clean
Summer clothes. Our hearts were thumping in our breasts.

I wanted to punctuate or somehow refute my own
Breathing. Messengers on push-bikes seemed to float
Through the haze like false witnesses for hire.

There was work, and there were forms of recreation
Enjoyed by brooding men: their anxious, sun-
Struck eyes scoured the environs for taxis.

My mind — had it been weighed — would have been
About the mass and density of an old-style association
Football. The scar across my forehead was the lace.

We were a long, swirling punt from the names
And numbers sewn into our garments: our milky
Reflections kept merging and dispersing in mirrors and
    doorways.

Every team learns to ignore its desperadoes; it was,
However, as yet unclear who would be chosen
To double back through the streets in search of help, or
    directions.

THE LONG MAN

of Wilmington winces with the dawn; he has just
endured yet another mythical, pointless, starry
vigil. His ankles ache, and the weather looks
irksome and moody; the early traffic whizzes by
regardless, but the news and emblems borne
by each car permeate the soil that sustains
the straggling furze, various grasses, and the odd
towering oak. Across the damp fields a distant
siren pleads for attention; he cannot
move, nor, like a martyr, disprove the lie of the land.

Who was it who established, in the teeth
of so much evidence, the laws of diminishing
returns? I woke up feeling cold and distended,
my feet pointing east, my head in low-hanging
clouds. A stream of curious tags and sayings
flowed like a potion through my veins. I had
the 'look', as some called it, meaning I floated
in an envelope of air that ducked and sheered
between invisible obstacles. The alarmed
senses struggled to respond, then bewailed
the absence of detailed, all-powerful
precedents: I kept picturing someone tracing
a figure on the turf, and wearing this outline
into a path by walking and walking around
the hollow head, immobile limbs, and cavernous torso.

LIVING WITH EQUATIONS

As I emerged from my hip-bath it suddenly dawned
The facts might be remarshalled and shown to rhyme.

Now the era need never end: its coefficients learn
To crack their knuckles, or reach for a handful of silver.

I watch the entangled sums unspool, as if the weight
Of earth pressed fitfully upon their mad proposals.

Stray hints lead across perilous forecourts, around
Noisy corners, then out into featureless, sandy scrub.

The devolved particulars — a shoe, a mole — reappear
In compounds that seem so explicit one forgets to gasp.

The remainder can only imperceptibly dwindle, retreating
Backwards until their long lost premises turn inside out.

JACK RABBIT

Will I ever catch up, or will I be easily
Caught first? It was assumed I'd branch out
With the heretics, commit a few crimes, then
Suffer the decreed punishment: instead, I paused
Near the knoll where the vociferous and well-
Groomed gather to consider their options. I yearned
To wade through buttercups and clover towards
The sinister squadrons of an embattled
Bourgeoisie. Vivid mottoes — *One Size Fits*
Nearly All!, No Grammar, No Furniture!, Le Temps
Viendra! — still adorn the half-built walls. Prodigal
Sons and daughters stream forth in search
Of business, clutching their coats, bewildered by doubts
And strange aches; a thin layer of soot powders the buildings
They pass, and the cracked bark of the peeling plane-trees.

*

So I reckoned to get quicker, leaner, braver, more
Self-effacing; I'd pick my way between
The mounds of junk cast off by warring factions, cleverly
Disguised and idly humming. I swam mid-stream
With the freshwater boys, and lounged on rocks
At evening. Meanwhile the air slowly thickened
With intrigue. Blueprints and memoranda
Began to circulate like the seasons, melting
The obdurate, blossoming where least expected:
We were to police ourselves, produce
Solemn recommendations, fall on our own

Swords. Wishes were transfigured into parables
And omens. Neither threats nor Chinese burns
Demolished my cloudy strategies, though a tow-haired
Bullyboy still slouches at the edge of sight, killing time.

EARLY TO BED, EARLY TO RISE

It was in Berlin you mixed up John and J. J. Cale,
And we found ourselves watching Jacques Tourneur's *Out
   of the Past* yet again.

I, on the other hand, confused Teniers the elder and Teniers
   the younger
In Amsterdam, where I saw Terry Gilliam's *Twelve Monkeys*
   on my own.

On the outskirts of Moscow we failed to distinguish clearly
   between Charles and Burl Ives;
Our punishment was to sit through Sergei Eisenstein's *Ivan
   the Terrible*, Parts I and II, twice.

I met a man in New York who couldn't tell the difference
   between George
And Zbigniew Herbert: his favourite film was Kenji
   Mizoguchi's *Ugetsu Monogatari*, which he insisted we see
   together.

In Cardiff I confounded Edward, Dylan, and R.S. Thomas;
To get over my embarrassment I went to a performance of
   Jean-Luc Godard's *Alphaville*.

People continually mistake the work of Antoine Le Nain for
   that of his brother Louis, even in Los Angeles,
Where most films are made, including Doug Liman's *Swingers*,
   which I recently saw for the first time, and really enjoyed.

MISGUIDED ANGEL

Where will you ride in this minute that stretches
Its wings, and soars aloft, and turns into
An unplanned, devilish interval? Serial
Misadventures have shattered the grip
Of barbed rubric and corporate logo; enigmas
Swarm at the brink of the five senses. When revealed
Each unlikely event exacts the stipulated
Blood-money, bequeaths boils and frets and fresh
Starts. Whirled from place to place and buffeted
By cross-winds, the sorrowing imp struggles on, gloomy
As the impending thunderheads: — Reflect, he insists,
On these peculiar facts: there is no controlling
One's renegade thoughts, nor striking
The fetters from blistered limbs. Inflexible etiquette
Demands every gesture be also a memory: you stare
Into space where fractions and figures still pursue
Their revenge; half-veiled by fumes, a lurid
Sickle moon unsettles the foundering traffic. Whoever claims
A stake out there must rise and speak in guttural tones
Of all they mean — or meant — to do, and why, and where.

HOOKED

then thrown back, like a long-finned, too bony
fish, I finally took
him at his word, and felt the lateness
of the hour acquire a dense, rippling
aura that weighed down these eyelids, pressed

apart membrane and nerve: howsoever I twist
and retreat, I thought, or silently glide from
sphere to sphere, the merest
splinter of rage keeps returning as a glittering, razor-
edged weapon, and even after dawn

has tightened still further the angle between
reflex and use, a sort of sunken
tide pushes open my ducts, washes through
or else over uncertain
crumbling defences, dissolves into itself whatever

floats, like quicklime, filters the air through fluids thicker,
    heavier
than water…as in a riddle, my entire
active vocabulary scatters and drifts, sucked
under, worn smooth to the touch; instead, circling
cries and swirling, opaque

graffiti scrawled in black
clouds of enormous letters come to seem
to define only their own unforgiving

and yet volatile laws: 'Thou
yet behold'st me?' I'm half-inclined to bellow in jest

at the elements, but decide, inversely, my first
real manoeuvre must
be to conceal from the inquisitive, lopsided sun
the direction in which these currents are secretly
driving me, and the immaculate, tiny

moons that now cover my body.

'WHEN I HEARD...'

after Charles d'Orléans

When I heard the alarm
Urging us to gather may
I made no effort to stir
To lift my head from the pillow
Saying to myself, it's early
I may as well sleep on
When I heard the alarm.

Young people share their finds
Unconcern is my friend
I'll share with him forever
He, he was my neighbour
When I heard the alarm.

I WISH

you would please spare me your Western logocentrism!
Isn't it clear I'm the sort who rejoices when the Queen Mother
chokes on a fish-bone? I'd shine a harsh,
piercing light on the damage indiscriminately wrought
by the tinkling music of the spheres. Our errands merely *seem*
average and natural: every second is underwritten
by an invisible host of dubious connections; like phantoms
they flit and soar, then render unto Caesar what is Caesar's.

Others — I am not the first — have found themselves standing
on a seemingly solid patch of cliff that suddenly
starts to slide: as the knees tense and the hips swivel, the
      winding
path is transformed into a slalom. Through a blizzard of loam
and pebbles, oaths and jests, I tumbled towards the
      proverbially
treacherous soft landing. A flock of seagulls squawked
and fled, and I remembered a man who claimed he could
      speak
their language fluently: 'Screeek!' he'd wail, 'Screeek, screeek!'

As any newsagent will explain, it is only, alas,
when their businesses collapse en masse that they
themselves are the news. The public-spirited tear
open the serrated pages in search of names
long wreathed in puzzling, clinging mists, now ablaze
with fame. The print smudges the fingers. Streams
of disjointed syllables cleave the air, and threaten
the passer-by who passes by, wrathfully, without flinching.

REPRODUCTION

of whatever you are absorbing with your
five senses is forbidden, and may provoke
nausea, insomnia, loss of balance or blurred
vision: it were better you retire, and then
attack, hurling weapons and imprecations
at the diffident foe. The world averts
its gaze, and unfortunate schemers drag
their woes from home to muddy fields: all
roads lead to rooms, as the Irish say, and
to windows through which one stares at the seething clouds.

One Indian summer, when the future
seemed to beckon with a double-jointed
finger, I took to loitering with uncertain
intent in the neutral, unblinking eye
of a slyly angled closed-circuit security
camera: when I yawned or stooped, somewhere
my grainy image followed suit. Shoppers paused
and threw me quizzical, sidelong glances. I perched
defiantly on the rim of a huge stone tub
of ferns, which I remembered, as they brushed my hair,
were thought by some to be about the oldest plants
on the planet. A portly, middle-aged
man in uniform, sporting mirror shades, ambled
towards me: I could tell he was bothered by the unseasonable
weather by the way my own features stretched and loomed.

HE AIMS

his catapult, and broods. Quivering washing
festoons the neighbouring gardens, and the sky lours
like a rival consortium, poised to swoop. 'Be

afraid' is his weird sort of motto. At dusk
clear divisions unfurl and dissolve; deluded
insects plunge frantically into pools and wedges

of soft, dizzying light. Scaly, half-formed scabs
begin to itch, then burn. The argument flies either
over the hedge, or from A to B and back again.

    ★

As a child's tongue probes a wobbly milk-tooth,
one is drawn to the far-flung, imperishable scenes featured
in a company calendar: veldt, ice-floes, desert, miles

of prairie. Under the gentle aegis of a wide-
angled lens, earth and sky exchange elaborate
favours. The greyish remains of an unlucky midge

streak the aureate canyons of Death Valley. A herd
of startled antelope gallop into the sunset: out
of frame a lion pursues, because his name is lion.

    ★

The conflict never ends, though the crowd chants
for a while before filtering home. The seasons revolve,
bringing honour and disgrace; flickering strings of price-

sensitive data orbit the world like molten, almost
invisible meteors. Look up and tremble: while the tongue
slurs and mangles yet more, ever-vaguer

resolutions, the body is taking its ten, horribly
deliberate paces. Eventually, if only to break
the eerie silence, he turns, closes both eyes, and fires.

PART II

And through a Riddle, at the last —
Sagacity, must go —

Emily Dickinson

TWENTY TWENTY VISION

Unwinding in a cavernous bodega he suddenly
Burst out: — Barman, these tumblers empty themselves
And yet I persist; I am wedged in the giant eye
Of an invisible needle. Walking through doors
Or into them, listening to anecdotes or myself spinning
A yarn, I realize my doom is never to forget
My lost bearings. *In medias res* we begin
And end: I was born, and then my body unfurled
As if to illustrate a few tiny but effective words —
But — oh my oh my — avaunt. I peered
Forth, stupefied, from the bushes as the sun set
Behind distant hills. A pair of hungry owls
Saluted the arrival of webby darkness; the dew
Descended upon the creeping ferns. At first
My sticky blood refused to flow, gathering instead
In wax-like drops and pools; mixed with water and a dram
Of colourless alcohol it thinned and reluctantly
Ebbed away. I lay emptied as a fallen
Leaf until startled awake by a blinding flash
Of dry lightning, and the onset of this terrible thirst.

TAKE THESE CHAINS

Authority would develop when things
Were done properly, or so you claimed, laughing
Like a flooded drain. These black leather, all-
Weather jackets repel both frost and fire; their zips
And buckles defend our motives from each other.

Now all and sundry declare that I ought
To have peeled away light-years before, while my
Markers were absent or dozing. *Au*
Contraire, I protest: I mean to double, nay,
Treble my winnings before I'm finished, you curs!

Grim fortune favours the disgruntled, whether
They be stick-in-the-muds or drifters; adjusting
To pain, the survivors slide forward on silent
Castors; I tear through the whole crowd,
Spurning friends, bare-faced rogues, and bemused strangers.

BRINKMANSHIP

In theory we choose our own criminals, she'd
Murmur into an unwitting ear: — and the supreme
Pontiffs of the city centre, or whoever fits
The bill had better take heed: we're here to shave
Them close, then closer still. Let them enjoy
Life up on the ledge while they may: wheeling
Construction cranes peck and jab at the turreted
Skyline. The stations never close. Power surges
Down the cables that connect the vehement
To the wavering and ill at ease. Our insignia
Are everywhere: it's like having wings, or moving
Through time and air as if each mirrored the other.

*

Men, historically, forswear their special friends
And worry instead about the territory stretching
Between themselves and the border. Their entrails
Warn of merciless reprisals; they love
Gouging lines in the fierce, rock-hard
Sand. New dilemmas beget old adventures, or vice
Versa, reducing all words to a wild musical
Growl in the throat. The errant protagonist
Strolls to and fro, and learns his own mind as he
Battles the wind and curses temptation; body
And spirit tear apart, scatter like sticky seeds caught
In the fur of animals, or the soft feathers of birds.

SHE SPEARS

a tender asparagus shoot, nibbles at intervals, then embarks
on an equivocal theory of what happened and why: — It was
    as if
I were — to borrow the title of a lurid thriller — *déjà*
dead! I sank through layers of debris and deceit, gnawed
by regrets, in search of a viable interiority. All around,
weeds sprouted in plant-pots: threads of cuckoo-spittle
dangled from thick-veined leaves that had outgrown
their strength. As I fell, the severed nerve in my right
ring finger began to tingle, then ache; *my eyes*, as I
    remembered
writing, almost dazed by my own cleverness, in my first
story at school, *slowly grew accustomed to the gloom* ...

What one sees — more or less — one finally gets, provided
it nearly fits, and is affordable: my funny body
still behaves like a brand plucked from a huge, fiercely
burning brazier. Just out of range, jocular opinion-
makers fiddle knowingly with their nostrils, and seem to
    think
they are immortal; a few ill-fated manoeuvers
later, I return to my booth, feeling neutral, neither sadder
nor wiser, but anxious about my jabs — tetanus, influenza
etcetera — and the laws of the jungle. According
to Flaubert, it is the various *mélancolies du voyage*, its
    piercing
disappointments which most exhilarate the true traveller.

Be that as it may, I found myself drifting from inner
suburb to inner suburb, without a car or pets, aside
that is, from sluggish clothes-moths and faithful silverfish:
jug-eared *La Vieille*, my least favourite landlady, took
to calling me in jest the Empress of the Reef. During this time
even casual jibes, or tiny acts of spite, used to make
me weep. One rainy morning, the mirror brutally informed me
that (a) anything went, and (b) one wrong move and I'd have
     no
moves left at all. The moment, I knew, had come to wreak
revenge on the glass, to watch my pupils diminish to dark
floating stars, to leave only the room in the reflection.

PENUMBRA

Beneath an angular web of scratchings-out
Vagrant motives glow like phosphorus: low, creeping
Tactics deny or dissolve whatever lies
In their path. I lean into the wind that blows
Off the lake, and scours the sodden fields; the sky's
Reflections ripple between ruts and bumps. I plunge
Towards remote vanishing points, where one man's
Loss unravels and becomes another man's
Devastation. Streams of ravaged spores dip
And swirl, and disappear, while downy
Nettles shiver beside a bristling hedge. Crops,
Sludge, restless drifts of leaves absorb
The haggard light. Things ready themselves for a reckless
Leap of faith: as storm-clouds hurry above the shadowy
Tree-line, the contours between grow vexed and dim.

WE CRAVE

attention, then come over all coy, and start fiddling
with watchstrap and buttons, or talking about a friend
of a friend who claims to own the world's largest collection
of aquarium ornaments, yet has no aquarium. In the mean-
time the tough-minded argue each of us is loved not
so much for his or her oddities, as in spite of them, or even
faute de mieux! Families form, squabble on long
car journeys, invent nicknames for strangers; the tyres hum
their own tune, and in shimmering forecourts
the baked atmosphere presses from all sides, searing
the lungs. We commend, internally, the wisdom of the soft-
voiced tycoon who acquired the land, only
to flatten it, then skilfully divide it into distinct
yet related lots; a spongy layer of wood-chips lines
the criss-crossing paths, and whispers faintly underfoot.

As it was drummed into me, I would drum it
into others: the art or science of management never
pauses, though it occasionally lies low, or enacts
retreat like a Parthian archer. Invariably, speed and stealth
take advantage of the famous, non-existent 'margin' poor
Herbert Pocket kept urging upon Pip; a sound decisive
as the whirr and double click of a computer mouse
signals the arrival of the inner bailiffs, and an era
of thrift. Listen harder, and through the virtual prison-bars
comes swarming the buzz of creditors and debtors over
lunch, each pledging allegiance to the other, to knowledge,
to the mysteries of living on thin air …

SHEEP'S HEAD GULLY

After years on the trail I could barely
Distinguish friend from enemy: they lay
Together like pebbles, immune to the seasons,
While I tramped about collecting odd remnants, ingesting
Their knowledge of knowledge. God-fearing bandits agreed
To disdain this porous earth that yields up nothing but itself
To bewildered intruders. Whispers drift
Across the sapping wastes, the clefts and lizard-like
Ridges; creepers flicker in the passing breeze; heaps
Of chalky bones reveal how some died
In their footsteps, land-hungry, scheming, at long last
Resigned. There proved no turning back, and hope
Came to seem the jaws of a lurid, furious monster
Glowering from the shadows. I notice that my right hand
Is cradling my left, and how the sky arcs
Overhead. In the distance crows wheel
Above each other in ever-shifting formations;
A glaucous haze envelops the scrub
Beyond, and seems to beckon like a vast sieve in which
I must shed my coat, my trappings, the scarf about my throat.

ONE FIGURES

in his plans, but briefly, as a cupped hand
holds water, or as private and public spheres collide

and blur, overlap within his fragile, omnivorous
stare. Barely awake, dazed and blinking, I was urged under

solemn oath to consider the lilies of the field who neither
toil nor spin. *Hallelujah*, I meant to answer, *selah*, only

a seething, surf-like roaring in my ears seemed to engulf
then drown both question and pause; twitching

open the drapes I glimpsed the faint sodium halo
of a street lamp through a tangle of jagged, spiny boughs.

      ★

I hate to lie, but unfortunately have come to loathe
the insatiable, unsheathed claws of truth; secret

forms of relation emerge, are brooded over
by the elect, then used to sell cars, newspapers, cosmetics

and sportswear. Contrarily, a sort of giddiness
rages in the veins of the innocent bystander, who leans

or shuffles ever closer, flushed and starry-eyed. Bruised
ex-lovers warn things will get harder, darker before

abruptly ceasing: in obscure, fiery runes each must learn
like Belshazzar, how to be numbered, weighed, divided.

      ★

So be it; as the sun dips behind the stadium, behind
minaret and mosque, a droning police helicopter banks

and circles, banks and circles: unnerved, an urban
vixen pokes her elegant muzzle skywards, deliberates,

then abandons her scavenging. Chapter and verse
yield to the harsh will of commentators, who rebuke

us all for invading the distance between soil and words,
hunger and clouds. In revenge, the rudiments — Balloo's

simple bare necessities — keep flowering into puns
that both induce double vision, and demand perfect balance.

  *

One falls, another clings like a fruit-fly to a shivering
nearly tangible cobweb of discounts, evasions

and regrets; on narrow inspection it transpires, further, our
unique covenant is open to the winds, and all

but illegible after dark. Blown about, drenched
to the bone, I keep returning to certain perilous clauses in fine

print that appear to refer, through a species of anagram, to my
wanderings and fears. Pinch me, pinch me, we hear ourselves
  murmur

over and over, as fierce measures are fervently called for
and taken, inscribed first in blood, then chiselled in stone.

THE CASKET

after Apuleius

'But — now listen! — on no account open this casket, however
Curious you may feel, Psyche, after it has been filled with
    divine beauty.'

So spoke the inspired, prophetic tower. Psyche made her way
To Taenarus where she obtained a pair of coins for the
    ferryman, and the required
Barley cakes soaked in wine and honey. There she began her
    descent
To the underworld: as the tower had instructed, she ignored
The lame drover and his hobbling donkey, made Charon
    take his obol
From her tongue, stopped her ears to the cries of the dead
Swimmer, spurned the crafty weavers at work
On their infernal looms, then soothed three-headed Cerberus
    with one
Of her sweet, dripping cakes. Finally she arrived at the palace
Of Proserpine, where she would not relax on the cushions
    the Queen
Proffered, and declined all food but a hunk of coarse, black
    bread. Squatting
At Proserpine's feet, she explained her commission from
    Venus; at once
The casket was whisked away to be filled in secret, then
    returned,
Sealed. On her swift journey back she used her other barley
    cake

To silence the rabid jaws of Cerberus, and again made hell's
   ferryman
Accept his payment from her mouth. But on regaining the
   white
Light of day she so adored, Pysche, although eager
To fulfil the task Venus had set her, suddenly fell prey
To temptation. 'I must be mad,' she mused, 'to carry, like
   this,
Beauty, and not take a little for myself, to please my divine
   lover.'
Accordingly, she opened the box, but found inside, not
   beauty,
But nothing, or rather an evil, insidious coma, a thick
Cloud of drowsiness which suffused and invaded her limbs
   until she collapsed
Where she stood on the path, and there she lay, slumped like
   a corpse, fast asleep.

YOU MUST

endeavour to abstain from these — he paused, and smiled —
indulgences: the market expresses the collective will
of traders who have lived through ravening epidemics,
tempests and droughts. What look to the newcomer
like loopholes turn invariably, in time, into elegant
Venus's flytraps; some greenhorn is forever
decrying the delicate equilibrium that makes possible
the flow of goods and events. Confine your accounts
to terse columns of figures marching sternly
into the wilderness, away from grieving family and friends.

I slept under strips of frayed curtain, in a room
that lacked furniture, and resembled a false-
bottomed suitcase; at length I relaxed, only
then to discover how many of my treasured, once
chronic ailments had either blistered or burst. Without
benefit of clergy the familiar and the unknown
kept colliding, and issuing ultimatums, like a pair
of generals at war in a crumbling grammar: 'Let battle
be joined; our envoys have returned empty-handed;
the enemy will sooner die than submit to the yoke.'

What is more, within the year, each and every hopeful
ends up learning never to answer questions posed
in letters, and how to turn the other cheek, or sharply
on one's heel. In late spring, cockroaches stir
and swarm from house to house: costly, futile
efforts are made to curb their sallies. Debts and profits
accumulate, each driving the imagination to expand

into distant, untouched regions. One shivers
or sweats, as the seasons break and fronds and tendrils
turn into wallpaper, and wallpaper into tendrils and fronds.

ARROWHEADS

Spring rain seeps
          between leather
                    upper and sole,
                              darkens the scabs
                                        of rust lining
                                                  the crevices
                                                  of a green Hillman
I say 'I', yet all I am is a spectre haunting some weedy, abandoned estate.
                                        order on behalf of the
                              a voice called for
                    like sea-birds until
               milled and cawed
          nephews and nieces
     cousins, distant
Brisk, ebullient

                                        it here: Horatio!
                              but will practise
                    I find this difficult
               by his first name;
          to address him
     begged me twice
     R— has now
Mister was her *nom de plume*, or rather spray-can, the police revealed.
     Mister he might
          have been called
                    for he was an old-
                         style outlaw,
                                   a saddle and trigger-
                                        happy hero, the last
                                             genuine *hombre.*

SNAGS AND SYNDROMES

Our collective reverie, a lost soul ventured
To explain, is about as random as the ebb
And flow of the stock exchange: we're so easily
Suckered we no longer care. The head and ears
Throb incessantly, and our spoofs and ripostes
Either fall flat, or degenerate into pleas
For sympathy. It becomes clear that each flaw, from
The structural to the trivial, must end up taking
The shape of a triangle: our schemes sink
Into the marl like arrowheads, then rear
As Satan in a pyramid of fire. Under duress, our
Verbs stammer and yield to an unknown third person
    singular.

              *

Ignoring all this, I sauntered forth, past a dog
Rattling his chain, autumn crocuses, vacant benches,
And tree trunks scarred with initials. A blue, dripping wet
Bag winked in the arms of a sycamore; squirrels
Worried among twigs and roots half-hidden
By twitching leaves. Someone, I noticed, had drawn
Boxes for hopscotch, then left the chalk itself
Lying in the penultimate square. Continuing, I stumbled
Upon the 'main drag', to borrow a term
Of my mother's. Cars, shops, and pedestrians merged
Into one: I heard my name whispered fiercely, excitedly,
In a voice I both dreaded and instantly recognized.

INSIDE

There are wheels within wheels, he yelled
At the wall, and within those wheels
Are tiny images, untitled books, desperate
Or creepy entanglements. The arrow-headed cursor points

Into space, but glides like a shark between
Sandbar and reef: I think of the pods, the soft
Fissured matter that makes up the brain, and how
Lightning forks and tears through swollen

Layers of cloud, burns like a tattoo in a far corner
Of the retina; reeling, in a cross-eyed
Fleeting trance, I'd feel I peered through jagged, hair-line
Cracks in air into streams of spiralling, contagious fire.

*

November 3rd. Cast aside all fears, all inhibitions
And *worked*. Also — but neutrally — happened to remember
Today is the anniversary of our long forgotten *neue*
Leben: having dipped first a toe, then my entire

Being in pure solvent, I am either
Numb as wood, or myself pure spirit. Mid-
Morning I paused, and heard the sharp clippety-clop
Of a police horse's hooves suddenly drowned by a car

Alarm's wailing. Left alone, inclined never
To complain to doctor, landlady, salesperson

Or lawyer, it is only in theory that I've no
Time or money, am open like a street map to the enemy.

    *

A new regime, supposedly, and even darting, bright-feathered
Rumour is lost for words, fidgets and flutters, each
Shifty eye pleading for shelter; in a prolonged fit
Of absent-mindedness I end up conceding point

After point, unable to resolve how to stem or else
Ride the ruthless, intricate currents as they
Flood then recede, burying the nerves under layers
Of heavy silt, sand, pollen, and rotting leaves. Another

Squinting sun, another set of assumptions to watch quiver
And disband: while fragments of a searing, inadmissible
Question blister the tongue, earth and air appear
Fused in a permanent dusk, the hour *entre chien et loup.*

'STOP KNOCKING...'

after Charles d'Orléans

Stop knocking for entrance to my thoughts
Care and worry, spare your knuckles,
For my brain is sleeping, and not to be woken —
Last night, you see, was spent in pain.

I must relax or I'll succumb, brain-fevered,
Please, please allow this poor mind rest.
Stop knocking for entrance to my thoughts
Care and worry; spare your knuckles.

As a cure Bon Espoir has devised
And had prepared a certain medicine:
I cannot lift my head from this pillow
Until I've had, at last, enough sleep sleep sleep...now
Stop knocking for entrance to my thoughts.

THE NIGHTINGALE'S CODE

She attempts a smile; the current tears at the stones
That strew its course, while overhead odd, waxy
Foliage glints in the sun. Beyond the grove voices
Are calling, calling the strayed members of numberless flocks:
They arrive, pock-marked and sleepless, muttering about
Ruin, and the tricks played by morning, and long
Forgotten routines. Our maps disagreed, until now
Only the awful and vacant remain yet
To be prised apart. I'd turned for home, hardly
Daring to breathe, as the highlighted zones declared war
On their meddlesome neighbours. I'd learned that silence
Lies in wait, then leaps to shroud the furniture. Grimacing,
The vowels retire, mass gloomily on the far
Horizons, where chalk and sand prepare to unfold
Their stiffened arms, to offer up their restive secrets.

NOTES

The *rondeaux* 'When I heard . . .' and 'Stop knocking . . .' are versions of 'Quant j'ai ouy le tabourin' and 'Ne hurtez plus à l'uis de ma Pensée' by Charles d'Orléans (1394–1465).

'The Casket' is based on an episode in Book VI of *The Golden Ass* by Apuleius (*c*. 125–*c*. 180).